HOW TO BREAK INTO THE WHITE HOUSE

Lots of

love,

Annie

AN IRREPRESSIBLE SMALL-TOWN GIRL'S
UP-CLOSE AND PERSONAL TALE OF
PRESIDENTS, GANGSTERS AND SPIES

HOW TO BREAK INTO THE WHITE HOUSE

ANN BRACKEN

Biteback Publishing

First published in Great Britain in 2021 by
Biteback Publishing Ltd, London
Copyright © Ann Bracken 2021

ISBN 978-1-78590-648-0

10 9 8 7 6 5 4 3 2 1

A CIP catalogue record for this book is available from the British Library.

Set in Minion Pro and Gotham

Printed and bound in Great Britain by
CPI Group (UK) Ltd, Croydon CR0 4YY

MIX
Paper from
responsible sources
FSC® C020471
FSC
www.fsc.org

To Alexander and Robin.

CONTENTS

1

A MIDWESTERN EDUCATION

I grew up in a small, one-horse town everyone makes fun of, described by comedian Steve Martin as 'the armpit of America'. In the United States, Muncie, Indiana, attracts almost as many jokes as Peoria, Illinois, or Hicksville, USA. The state is as flat as a pancake. The cornfields around us were straight out of the crop-duster scene in the movie *North by Northwest*. The Indians had long since been exterminated – apart from one or two propping up the local bars.

Though in my teenage years I started to dream of broader horizons, I always go back to visit where I came from. My friends elsewhere in America and Europe seem a bit shocked at hearing that I come from one of the 'fly-over' states in Middle America, which they tend to regard as primitive and beyond the pale. They do represent an entirely different, older and sometimes saner country – for New York and Los Angeles, despite the fascination they exert elsewhere, could hardly be less representative of the US as a whole. The states and people in the heartland are more attached to traditional values, less 'progressive', more conservative, patriotic, reverential about the military and down to earth. Dinner in Indiana is at 6 p.m., sometimes 5.30. Transgender issues are not high on the agenda. We are a corn state with lots of cattle. We are really good at what we do, which is agriculture, causing the European Union and other jurisdictions to erect all sorts of barriers to keep our produce out. We can supply enough to help overcome famines by sending our crops anywhere we have the chance to.

A high proportion of the population end up

weighing around 300 pounds. But those who do visit will tell you about their hospitality, their will-ingness to help neighbours and their unfeigned friendliness. No one is looking for a job on Wall Street to practise shorting or invest in CDOs squared (whatever they are) in an effort to bring down the world financial system. Wall Street and Washington are not trusted by them. They prefer small government to big and are quite pleased when elections result in deadlock in DC, on the grounds that it may then do less harm. There is a tendency to believe in the Almighty and lower taxes. On an aircraft recently, I took my seat next to a typically enormous denizen, wearing a T-shirt that, on the front, said: 'In God we trust'. On the back it said: 'Everyone else gets searched'.

My family more or less owned the town, or at any rate the major glassmaking factory there, and they founded the university and the hospital. Ahead of David Letterman, the university's most illustrious alumnus is the Garfield creator, Jim Davis. Davis had such a profound influence on me that we now own a cat that looks and behaves exactly like

Garfield, though without the charm. He even tries to steal the dog's food and water. The dog is a beautiful, gentle but unfortunately brainless blonde who fails to defend herself against these ruthless attacks.

To get back to my origins, my parents naturally decided that only my brother needed to go to a worthwhile school and prestigious university, whereas I had the benefit of a public school education which has led people to make fun (rightly so) of my spelling ever since. Public school in the US means exactly what it says, unlike in Britain, where it means the opposite.

My grandparents lived in a huge mansion, built with the profits from the tens of millions of fruit jars they sold in the Second World War. My grandmother threw parties for the surrounding citizenry, which my grandfather did not enjoy. He was known to hide behind the curtains in the living room during receiving lines with only his shoes sticking out, pretending not to be there.

The other patriarch in the family was my great-uncle, Ed Ball, who served with distinction with General Mark Clark in North Africa and Italy in the Second World War and remained a close buddy of his after the war. He and a friend took their wives out for a boat ride and, unfortunately, blew them both up. Both men survived, but their wives, tragically, did not.

Though my grandmother claimed that her ancestors arrived in the US on the *Mayflower*, the family names are nowhere to be found on the passenger list. More credibly, however, the Balls can lay claim to a famous ancestor: Captain Alexander Ball of the Royal Navy. When blockading the French Mediterranean coast with Nelson in 1798, they were caught up in a violent storm that disabled Nelson's flagship, HMS *Vanguard*. To rescue Nelson and his ship, Captain Ball threw them a line. As they were driven ever closer to the French coast, Nelson ordered his lieutenant to save his own ship by cutting it, but Ball refused to do so, earning, as they then struggled clear, Nelson's fervent gratitude. But for Captain Ball, Nelson might never have been at the Battle of Trafalgar.

When I was still very young, my family moved to Washington, as my father became an aide to Wally

Hickel, the Governor of Alaska. Hickel had been appointed by the new President, Richard Nixon, to be Secretary for the Interior, including oversight of the national parks and environmental affairs. (The Environmental Protection Agency, believe it or not, was set up by Richard Nixon.) But Wally Hickel, who was much smarter than the rest of the administration, famously opined that the best thing to do in Vietnam was to declare victory and leave. This was not appreciated by the President, causing Hickel to make an early return to Alaska, where in due course he resumed serving happily as governor for many years.

Our neighbours in our cul-de-sac in Washington were a well-known family with presidential ambitions, and two of them actually did become Presidents. George H. W. Bush, President No. 41, used to try to embarrass me ever afterwards by telling the surrounding guests at receptions, 'I have seen this young lady with no clothes on.' Which indeed was true as, aged six, I cut my ankle in the bathtub and ran next door to appeal to him for help. This super-kindly man wrapped me in a blanket, rushed me to the hospital and stayed with me there until I could be released. He also was responsible for my early tennis training, letting me hit a ball on a string in his backyard. Not only that, it was Congressman Bush who taught me to throw an American football in a spiral, enabling me later to see off all rivals to become the quarterback for my Kappa Kappa Gamma sorority at the University of Michigan. I was less enthusiastic at this stage about President No. 43, as one night someone drove erratically down our cul-de-sac, squashing flat my poodle, Lollypop. An extensive cover-up followed with no admission of guilt and, in any case, we have got on very well since.

Back in Muncie, my father was a lawyer, but he was proud of having trained in his youth as a wrangler (cowboy). My farm girl credentials were enhanced by being instructed by him to 'take off like a runaway calf' so that he could practise lassoing me. Aged thirteen, I entered my orange hair phase and was determined career-wise to become a Disco Queen, for which I had, and still have, excellent qualifications. I dragged my very unfortunate, strait-laced WASP father to numerous performances of The Doobie Brothers, Fleetwood Mac, Billy Joel and The Police at which, despite some coughing, he failed to notice the surrounding haze of marijuana. I fell totally in love with The Police in general and with Gordon Sumner (alias Sting) in particular and have been trying to make contact with him ever since.

The orange hair phase led to numerous car accidents and various scrapes with the law, resulting in my father sending me to paramilitary training with Outward Bound. This was nearly the death of me, as I found myself spelunking deep underground in some dark and dodgy caves from which, one year later, a couple of other victims failed to return.

From this character-building exercise I returned with only a mild concussion, the result of a boulder falling on my head. I also got thrown overboard on a river rafting trip and stranded for a night on a mountain. Told to go out and hunt my own food for a couple of days, I experienced the most effective diet of my career.

Since even my parents recognised that I had

barely survived, next year I was despatched to teach at a tennis camp for spotty young kids, some older than me, where I was able to perfect my lethal backhand at their expense. Since at this point I was pretty hefty despite the Outward Bound regime, I had a Serena Williams-like effect on the opposition, ending up at one point as No. 3 in my age group in the Midwest. The competition was unfair, as the other two girls were even heftier than me.

In Muncie, in this period, on Saturday nights the local youth and I would gather to engage in our favourite pastime, which was cow tipping. This entails sneaking up on an unsuspecting cow sleeping upright in some farmer's field and tipping it over, a feat requiring considerable guile and skill.

These days I live in London, but some Brits can be a bit snooty and constipated. When I mention my prowess in this sport to them, they pretend to be horrified. The head of the Ministry of Agriculture turned ashen, clearly fearful that I might seek to popularise it in the Home Counties. All of which ignores the fact that the cows otherwise lead boring lives with no element of fantasy or surprise. They roll over and struggle back to their feet, none the worse for the experience and considerably smarter than they were before.

For their holidays my family collectively decided to colonise the area between Lake Michigan and the much smaller and more user-friendly Lake Leelanau, which they did so effectively it is now known as Indiana Woods. I spent many happy and educational hours waitressing in the local Michigan hostelries with names like Woody's and the Happy Hour. At Woody's, I remain quite famous for having carried a huge tray with a dozen long-neck beers and glasses over to a festive table, before depositing them in the laps of the customers. I mixed up orders on a regular basis, which added spice to people's evenings out, as they never knew what was coming next. The remuneration was disappointing, leading me to conclude that I had better find some other sources of income. (Recently, my other half has offered to pay me handsomely for washing his Aston Martin DB4, provided I dress up like Liv Tyler in *One Night at McCool's*, an offer I am still considering.)

A visit to my very expensive dentist in London's Cavendish Square to get my tusks burnished a frightening shade of white takes me back to the days when my dental treatment was by a Second World War veteran in Indiana, who would lean over me searching for cavities with a cigarette clenched firmly between his teeth. I didn't mind the occasional flakes of ash falling down my throat as he was extremely liberal with his use of laughing gas, which, to my dismay, appears to be illegal in the United Kingdom. Despite my entreaties, my very pukka London dentist keeps refusing to supply me with any.

While my brother headed from his swanky private school to Stanford, I graduated early from my high school in Muncie to study at the University of Michigan, home of the legendary Wolverines, America's most successful college football team. A 100,000-person stadium is required to cope with the attendance at home games. Former players include President Gerald Ford. Still chunky at the time, I persuaded the much sought-after quarterback to accompany me to a party, only for him to spend his time fraternising with slimmer female students (which proved a worthwhile lesson for me to learn).

Family holidays in this period were challenging, as my father did represent a bygone age. To be avoided was walking down a hotel corridor with him as, invariably, he would find somebody who had left a room service tray outside their room, trip over it, go sprawling and require resuscitation (which I have been struggling how to spell). The same applied to sailing, for this was liable to require, as it did in St Lucia, emergency rescue efforts to stop us crashing into the Pitons. And boating near our house in Michigan on Lake Leelanau. Not content with one ancient and beautiful Chris-Craft, the *Rosemary*, with which he kept making huge bow waves through the docking channel, causing other boatmen to panic, he acquired an even older version, which he hunted down in Arizona. The money spent restoring it was astronomical but in vain, as every single outing ended with it sinking slowly and elegantly beneath the waves.

My father was the sort of person who, standing

upright, would go down with his ship, but the lake was too crowded to allow this to happen and he was rescued repeatedly by interfering well-wishers. On the occasion when the rudder fell off after an unwise attempt at water-skiing, I plus my three-year-old child jumped off and swam across the lake. As soon as we had come to shore, an expectant crowd gathered, ready to dry us off and give us cups of hot chocolate.

Nevertheless, I loved my father, even though my patience was sorely tried by his technique as a tennis partner. He would crouch below the net, even though he was 6ft 4 inches tall, before jumping into the air like a jack rabbit and yelling 'Darn it!' (no blaspheming) as he missed the ball every single time, my mother rolling her eyes to the sky.

Three weeks' cycling across the misty forelands of Ireland was another character-building experience, with my father wearing a red bandana and refusing to shave. I preferred cycling past the châteaux of the Loire, especially Chenonceau, presented by the King of France to his girlfriend, a role model of mine, Diane de Poitiers. For Diane was as sporty as she was beautiful, famous for bathing nude in the lake, even in winter. Unfortunately, when the King died his widow, Catherine de Medici, confiscated the chateau for herself.

Although worth a good deal of money thanks to his ancestors, most of which he donated to nature conservancy, my father never was presented with a restaurant bill without failing to express shock, horror, outrage and disappointment at the amount. When I go out these days with my appointed escort, he is not allowed to protest in any way when given the bill, however astronomical it may be, as it often is in St Tropez or Cap Ferrat. I keep pointing out that I am a relatively cheap date, as I don't *do* lunch and a few years ago I gave up champagne in favour of Diet Coke.

• • •

In my senior year, I seized the chance to spend part of it with some of my classmates in an exchange programme in Greece. I climbed around the Acropolis, where construction began 2,000 years before the US even started to exist, enjoyed the now defunct village atmosphere of the Plaka and, of course, explored the islands. I developed an abiding enthusiasm for the Greek gods who, with their foibles and their rivalries, are so *human*. But our visits to the islands entailed being escorted by hordes of local youths making strange clucking noises. We had to lock ourselves in the bathrooms on every ferry. On the journey to Crete we were saved only by the intervention of the crew. We had to come back by air! A *sortie* to Cairo was beset by the same problems, only worse.

My first real job after graduating was with an aerospace company in Boulder, Colorado. In the foothills of the Rocky Mountains, Boulder had become a Mecca for those addicted to ultra-healthy living and extreme sports. I soon discovered that the city was inhabited by two types of men: professional or pseudo-professional athletes and engineers. I enjoyed my job in the public relations department, but my social life was somewhat lacking, as their and my idea of a date at the time was a ten-mile run, followed by splitting a bran muffin.

Due to some unwise self-advertisement, I was invited to join the ski racing team, who needed a woman to qualify for the slalom championship. My colleagues hurtled down the mountain, wiggling their butts as they weaved between the slalom gates. Then it came to my turn. I set off with equal confidence but, unfortunately, did not make the first gate or any other after that, leaving a row of flattened flags in my wake. I arrived to find the team disqualified, with my colleagues holding their heads in their hands. It took me a while to live this down.

Meanwhile, for part of my time in Boulder, I was seconded as a loan executive to the United Way, which at the time was the largest and best-funded charitable organisation in America. It was dedicated to building bridges across the different communities in the US and to helping those in most need. My job was mainly fundraising from corporate America, but I was enthusiastic about what we were trying to achieve.

To get back to my Midwestern roots, I hightailed

it back to Michigan to participate in what is claimed to have been the 100th extended family reunion, though my home state isn't really much older than that. Attended by a couple of hundred close relatives, this began ambitiously with an evening beach party, but had to be relocated to the Leland Country Club because of pouring rain. This was an utter disaster as the club turned out to be *dry*, causing a headlong rush of SUVs and pick-up trucks to the nearest bottle store.

Next day, there was some unseemly jostling to get into the front row of the family photo. This time at least, the event was not dry, but it proved impossible to get close to the buffet or barman because of several 300-pound relatives barring the way. This was followed by a barn dance at which pseudo rap songs and Indian pow-wows were performed indifferently by the paler members of the family, which seemed a pity because there definitely was the odd mixture of Native American and Afro-American ancestry in the good old days. To complete the festivities, my Grosse Pointe bankers then arrived to tell me that Detroit had gone bust and my world-famous financial institution was under criminal investigation.

Taking this in my stride, I challenged them to a winner-takes-all tennis match against my offspring and me on the following day, resulting in an epic struggle. A consultation with my partner was required to impress on him the consequences of losing. This led to a renewal of interest on his part and the narrowest possible victory in the tiebreak, following which we won the family championship without breaking sweat.

Throughout the family reunion my sister made me really mad by goading me about her numerous encounters with Sting backstage at Red Rocks in Boulder! Even though I crossed the Atlantic especially to meet him, I still haven't done so yet. After each one of these meetings she taunts me further by texting me photos of Sting with his arm around her or toasting her with a glass of red wine, causing further grief and pain. Under interrogation, it turns out that she is a friend of Sting's astrologer, on whom he is said to rely completely. She is refusing flatly to introduce me to the astrologer, let alone to Sting, all because I used to boss her around and make her and my other sister dress up as Sting for Halloween.

While in Boulder I decided that I must make a further effort to broaden my horizons. So, I enrolled to study for a degree in international relations at the London School of Economics. The teaching was excellent and I enjoyed the classwork. My life was complicated by the lodgings the college found for me with an impoverished single-parent family in Finsbury Park. My bed was in a closet and bathing was severely discouraged. My feeble protests were brushed aside on the grounds that nothing else was available. This did have the effect of making me explore London by walking everywhere, rather than return to my dire digs. And the LSE eventually obtained a secondment for me as assistant to the representative for Leicester in the European Parliament.

We set off regularly to the meetings in Brussels and Strasbourg. My impressions of the institution itself were not entirely favourable, I'm afraid. It was quite hard to figure out what it was there for, except to provide food and lodging for the hungry and thirsty delegates. The food and drink were excellent, which is more than could be said for the debates. The members seemed often to be disappointed politicians, the more ambitious ones having decided to stand for their national Parliaments. Nor was it clear who was listening to what was said there, especially of course in Britain, the Brits being particularly allergic to it. What got the members most excited were the plans for huge expenditure on vast new buildings, which in due course were built to house it.

2

INSIDE THE CAPITOL

From my vantage point in Europe, I watched the 1988 US election in alarm as George Bush, Vice-President to Ronald Reagan, trailed the Democrat Governor of Massachusetts by seventeen points in the opinion polls. But the Bush campaign in this election was run by the no-holds-barred Lee Atwater, who did not find it hard to portray Dukakis as, like his state, too 'progressive' and left-wing for Middle America, in which Atwater was aided by Willie Horton. Massachusetts had a penal system with generous furloughs for prisoners.

The Massachusetts legislature passed a bill barring convicted murderers from benefiting from this, but, as governor, Dukakis vetoed it. When Willie Horton, a black American convicted of murder, was released, he went on a rampage, including committing rape and other acts of violence. Dukakis was a fragile candidate, but Willie Horton sure didn't help. Bush won by a landslide. My parents and I were invited to the celebrations in Washington, where we saw a guitar-playing, cigar-chomping Lee Atwater performing a duet with the new President. Atwater tragically died from a brain tumour a couple of years later.

My father, who was an ardent conservationist, was hoping to serve in the new administration. As other candidates either failed to survive the vetting process or declined to put their wealth into blind trusts, eventually he got his wish to be appointed as the principal deputy to the Secretary of the Interior. This gave him full scope to wear his Civil War uniform much of the time, including sword and musket, which I think is illegal. A convinced Yankee, my dad would start crying immediately if anyone mentioned Gettysburg or Abraham Lincoln, and in fact made a long speech about Lincoln at my sister's wedding without ever mentioning the bride. As a result, I had to tramp over every Civil War battlefield on the eastern seaboard, often up to my shins in mud. We had a particularly memorable visit to Little Round Top in Gettysburg. First, we stayed in the local hostelry, the Cashtown Inn, where, as soon as night falls, you can hear the groans of 18,000 soldiers massacred on the battlefield (I presume the inn has a CD wired to frighten the guests). My uncle swore he was awakened by a huge crash outside his window and my mother also woke up in a sweat to crashing sounds.

To escape the horrible groaning, we decided to visit the battlefield after dinner in the pitch dark, with rain pouring down. As soon as we got close to Little Round Top, my father frog-marched us out into the darkness and locked the car doors with the keys inside. My uncle, a Purple Heart Korean War veteran, was scared to death, as he could hear ghosts whispering in the graveyard.

My mother and I, made of sterner stuff, were

too busy cursing my father in the pouring rain to worry about the neighbourhood spirits. Fortunately, we found a plucky young couple making out in a parked car nearby, a curious choice of venue for this kind of activity. We interrupted them for long enough to get them to tell the park ranger that his boss (my father was in charge of the National Parks) had locked his family out in a graveyard at midnight in the pouring rain. The ranger appeared unsurprised by this (my dad had a well-merited reputation for eccentricity) and, using his flexible coat hanger, managed to get us back in the car so we could go back to the Cashtown Inn and lie awake listening to the ghosts groaning there.

As I planned my own invasion of Washington following the inauguration, I knew that I could expect no help from the two people I knew best. My strait-laced father had not yet been appointed to the administration and – good for him – he would sooner have perished than lobby for a position for his daughter. As for the President, under no circumstances was I going to embarrass him or

To Annie Bracken —
With Appreciation a Best Wishes from
your former neighbor and from your friend   Gg Bush

With the President in the Oval Office. © The White House

Cowgirl in Indiana. Author's collection   Bracken family. Author's collection

At the University of Michigan. Author's collection

Graduation with my proud father. Author's collection

To Annie Bracken
With best wishes,
Gg Bush

With the President at the White House,
December 1989. © The White House

To Annie Bracken
With appreciation and best wishes,
Gg Bush

With the President at the White House,
December 1990. © The White House

*To Annie Bracken
With best wishes,* G Bush

Greeting the President and the Dutch Prime Minister in The Hague, June 1991. © The White House

*To Annie Bracken
With best wishes,*

With Vice-President Quayle. © The White House

THE PRESIDENT   September 25, 1992

Dear Annie,

Welcome back! I'm glad to hear that you enjoyed
your time in Holland and that you're now working on
the campaign. It's been a tough fight, but I'm
feeling confident and am grateful to have you on our
team. November is just around the corner -- we will
win!

Thanks so much for your upbeat letter. Please give
my best to your Mom and Dad. With warm regards,

saw your great Dad today in Chicago

Sincerely,

George Bush

A note from
the President:
'Welcome back',
September 1992.

Author's collection

THE PRESIDENT   December 9, 1992

Dear Annie,

Thanks so much for your kind note. Barbara and I
are grateful for the privilege **we have had** to serve
the American people and are **very proud** of our team.
Thanks for all you did for us.

We Bushes are now looking ahead and the sun is
rising. Back to Houston on January 20 and more time
with family and friends -- that's where you and your
mom and dad come in. I wish you lots of luck,
Annie, in whatever the future may bring. Have a
very merry Christmas!

Saw your Dad yesterday. Lookin' good

Sincerely,

George Bush

A note from
the President:
'Sorry we lost',
December 1992.

Author's collection

At John
Gardiner's
tennis ranch in
Carmel Valley.

Author's collection

Working in Manhattan. © Loic Bisoli

Rainbow Room. © Loic Bisoli

At the Union Square Café. © Loic Bisoli

Tennis at Queen's.
Author's collection

Surprising myself and a trout on the river Test. Author's collection

Pretending to be a Brit. Author's collection

myself by asking him for a post. I was utterly resolved to try to make my way in the capital under my own steam.

So, like all other newbies, I became a serf in the office of a legislator from my state, who needed a well-trained farm girl like me to lick envelopes for him. My duties included bringing the coffee, answering the phone, greeting constituents and jogging with the senator when required. I was soon upgraded to 'legislative correspondent', which entailed helping the senator to deal with his daily deluge of letters, either agreeing enthusiastically with expressions of support or starting replies with the words 'Reasonable people can disagree...' I did point out that this response was unlikely to work, as many of the people we disagreed with weren't reasonable at all. But at least all this was for the very accomplished senior senator from Indiana, Richard Lugar, deputy chairman of the Senate Foreign Relations Committee (the chairman, on grounds of even greater antiquity in the Senate, was the pretty awful ultra-right-wing Jesse Helms).

I had arrived full of enthusiasm for this great and powerful institution but was in for a few surprises. For ahead even of Helms in seniority was Senator Strom Thurmond, who, believe it or not, continued to serve in the Senate until he died at over 100. The majority leader, Senator Dole, used to advise adhering to the same diet as Thurmond: 'When he eats a banana, I eat a banana!' The ancient senator appeared to have been frozen in aspic by the time I got to the Capitol. He had to be carried into the Chamber and instructed how to vote by his aides. Having already married two Miss South Carolinas, in his dotage he attempted to get engaged to a third. Senator Robert Byrd also lasted until he was over ninety. Both had been ardent opponents of the civil rights movement. Byrd was a former member of the Ku Klux Klan, while Thurmond turned out to have fathered a black child.

But also at this time there were some senators on both sides of the aisle who were interested in bi-partisan compromise, Lugar being one of them. And the Democrats Dianne Feinstein (known as

Di-Fi) and Joe Lieberman were others. The Republican senator and Vietnam War hero John McCain actually wanted to make the Democrat Lieberman his running mate in the 2008 presidential election, but their respective colleagues wouldn't stand for it. What chance of success he had disappeared when he saddled himself with Sarah Palin from Alaska as his running mate instead.

The Wyoming senator Al Simpson's party piece was a speech about temperance. Having expounded on the beauty of water in the oceans, sparkling rivers and magnificent cloudscapes, he would conclude by declaring: 'But as a beverage, it ain't worth a damn.' Senator Burns from Montana told me that the advice he gave to younger colleagues was: 'Never squat when you're wearing spurs.' Less helpfully, at a party, the Republican senator for Illinois made flattering but highly inappropriate comments about my by now more sylphlike physique (a crash course with Weight Watchers and non-stop working out having caused me to lose some surplus kilos).

And then – yes, even then – there was Joe Biden,

who was, and based on a more recent encounter still seems to be, a really nice guy, whose opinions have changed over time. As he is about to be sworn in as President, you might like to know more about him, on which please see Chapter 8 of this memoir.

Before working on Capitol Hill, I had imagined that senators must live exciting and glamorous lives. Apart perhaps for John Warner, who was married (briefly) to Elizabeth Taylor before walking out with Barbara Walters, this proved to be anything but the case. I felt so sorry for my senator, who was a really good man but who had to spend by far the greater part of his time in non-stop fundraising and meeting the endless torrent of visitors from Indiana and from lobby groups with names like 'Beer Drinkers of America', all of whom insisted on personal encounters with him. He had also lost out for the vice-presidency to the uniquely unqualified (but better-looking) junior senator from his state. This could have made him permanently grouchy, but he was very nice to me when he could spare time from overthrowing the President and Imelda

Marcos in the Philippines (he objected very strongly to her world-class collection of over 1,000 pairs of designer shoes). His constituents, however, could scarcely have cared less what happened there.

3

INVADING THE
WHITE HOUSE

was bent on being upwardly mobile. Rather than
seeking promotion on Capitol Hill as an aide to
my senator, my sights were set much higher. It had
always been my intention to infiltrate the White
House. Nor, with the hubris of youth, did I believe
there was much chance of anyone being able to stop
me.

This required a sustained and well-planned
military-style campaign, over many months, to be-
friend everyone associated with the place. I found

an early chink in the institution's armour in (where else?) the secret service, members of which seemed pleased to have me join them on their daily midday jog around Capitol Hill. I became so chummy with them that, rather than scrutinise me, I got a warm welcome whenever I could find a pretext to get anywhere near the White House grounds. From another angle, my secret weapons included Katharine Graham, owner of the *Washington Post* and *Newsweek*. She was addicted to tennis but badly needed some help on the courts, which it fell to me to provide. She was banned from the White House by Barbara Bush, who never forgave her for a horrendous *Newsweek* cover that depicted her husband, a fighter pilot who had narrowly survived being shot down over the Pacific in the Second World War, as a wimp. The President would have forgiven her, but not for nothing was Barbara known, despite her grandmotherly image, as the Don Corleone of the Bush family. Still, Kay's parties were frequented by plenty of guests with White House connections, all blissfully unaware of my infiltration plans.

An early attempt at doing so appeared to have

failed, as I installed myself at dinner between two high-powered White House staffers who spent the entire evening talking politics to each other, totally oblivious to my charms. One of them, however, had second thoughts and called me the next day. I was impressed, as he was close to 7ft tall. This was important to me as, at 5ft 10 inches without my heels, I tend to tower over most men once I put them on. Not only that, as a member of the domestic policy staff, my new friend featured frequently as a talking head on the TV. He did have, it is true, some peculiarities. He lived on a regime of popcorn and Diet Coke. The apartment he rented near Dupont Circle still had all its furniture wrapped in plastic covers. Here, I had to watch the movie *Blade Runner* innumerable times (he was understandably obsessed with Daryl Hannah). His efforts to advance his cause with me included performing wild solo dances with whirling arms and feet amidst the plastic-covered furniture. He decided to undertake my political education by sending me each day, to improve my mind and apart from roses, selected articles and memos, all of which he had written himself. But what chances this relationship had of flourishing were quickly dashed, for as soon as I actually joined the White House staff he seemed to feel threatened (possibly rightly) and said he now had to devote all his slender leisure time to watching political talk shows.

Meanwhile, I had discovered from my contacts the amazingly high burn-out rate within the White House, especially among the junior staff. Arriving in Washington with high expectations, these unfortunates found themselves treated as barely paid serfs, working impossible hours and scarcely able to get back to their rented apartments to sleep. Within months, I reasoned, some of them would be bound to throw in the towel. Meanwhile, I got myself invited into the precincts, on various pretexts, to ceremonies such as the President pardoning the Thanksgiving turkey. I kept sending my CV to the Bureau of Presidential Personnel, responsible for all White House appointments, and, better still, got to know some of the denizens there.

My determination and dogged persistence paid off as, eventually, I was given a hard-earned and pretty gruelling interview, which sought to check on any compromising connections or other misdeeds on my part. After a further wait, one day a letter came back offering me, subject to security clearance, a position in… Presidential Personnel. The FBI set about interrogating everyone who had ever known me at college or in my youth in Muncie. Very much on their mind was whether I had ever smoked a doobie or ingested illegal chemicals (answer: no). They failed to find out about my orange hair phase, and I was granted security clearance up to Secret level! This seemed pretty weird to me, as my new role clearly was going to be an extremely humble one.

The next hurdle to overcome was that the White House does not have a proper budget, so virtually all the staff have to be paid by other institutions – in my case, to my surprise, the Environmental Protection Agency. I only had to go there once, just to register with them, but I didn't cost them much (less than $20,000 a year).

I was now, at last, duly registered as an assistant to the President and member of the White House staff. But the working space there is so tiny that hardly anyone beyond the chief of staff, his deputy, the national security adviser, the legal counsel, the head of Congressional Relations and the senior domestic policy adviser actually have offices in the West Wing. Across a narrow lane within the White House precincts lies the Old Executive Office Building, containing anyone of less than stratospheric status such as, for instance, the Vice-President and all his staff, the National Security Council (NSC) staff, the legal staff and, on the ground floor, Presidential Personnel.

I soon felt at home, as the Veep's staff were nearly all from Indiana. It would have been much easier for me to join them, but my ambition had always been to end up working for the President. When I achieved that, as I expected, I found myself at the very bottom of the food chain and everybody's gofer. While others might have been discouraged, I could see only the opportunity.

One of my tasks was to sift through applications for ambassadorships and assistant secretary positions in the administration and other presidential appointments, most of which had not yet been filled. Criterion No. 1 was: did they contribute to the President's campaign? Were there any red flags from the FBI (some quite interesting ones) or obvious conflicts of interest? Did the candidate have any chance of getting through the Senate confirmation process? As for the ambassadorships, the candidates needed to be wealthy contributors to the political campaign, preferably friends of the President, who could then pay for their own diplomatic entertainment, which the State Department did not have the funds to meet. My task was to put those who looked unable to meet those requirements on the discard list.

I was not allowed to lobby for who *should* be appointed, although I did so vigorously (along with everyone else) for Arnold Schwarzenegger as head of the Council for Physical Fitness. This earned me invitations to celebratory parties for him, at which we urged him to take up a political career – on the opposite side to his wife, Maria Shriver! The scary Terminator turned out to be absolutely charming. He went on to do very well as a two-term Republican Governor of California in the early 2000s.

Finding this activity otherwise unrewarding, I took charge of the interns' programme, as no one else was interested in them. These too were usually the sons and daughters of wealthy contributors. I arranged for them to visit the presidential plane, Air Force One, and engaged them to help set up for formal White House arrival and departure ceremonies. I kept them well away from the Oval Office, except for one group photograph. There was never the slightest chance of a Monica Lewinsky slipping the leash on my watch.

As my purple pass gave me access to the West Wing whenever I was needed, I made sure that I was needed more often than not. As General Scowcroft needed a new sofa for his office, it fell to me to charm the US Navy (who run the White House) into giving him one. With my troop of interns, I carried out such errands as arranging the chairs on the White House lawn for the visit of Queen Elizabeth. The ceremony did not work out quite as expected, as my friend, the head of protocol, positioned the microphone at what he thought was a suitable height, unaware that Her Majesty is barely 5ft tall. When the time came for her speech, all that could be seen of the monarch was her hat. This passed into White House folklore, and that of the Washington press corps, as the 'Talking Hat' speech.

There were numerous other opportunities to stroll around the White House or the grounds, taking care to be clad in attractive outfits. From time to time, I would receive a call not long after dawn summoning me to tennis with the President, his son, Marvin, and whatever dignitary was visiting at the time. Which is how I got to play with Pete Sampras who, fortunately, was handicapped by having the President as his partner. With no warm-up, snipers on the roof and the secret service in attendance, the understandably nervous and still very youthful Sampras actually mis-hit a couple of our balls! Following which, chided by the President, he single-handedly thrashed us; the Bush game, as with his golf, consisted of huge enthusiasm but not much accuracy. Playing golf on his friend Walter

Annenberg's course in Palm Springs, the President unfortunately struck the ball so hard and inaccurately that it laid out a lady in the attendant crowd.

Other early morning summonses were to go for a run with the President and his security detail. With the hyper-active George Bush Senior, these runs started before dawn, causing us on one occasion to have to pretend to admire the magnificent spring-time display of blossoms in Washington *when it was still dark.*

I had to get up at 5 a.m. to work out every day anyway, so as to keep in the right shape. On my infrequent early mornings off, my tennis partner was the legendary former head of the CIA Dick Helms. When President Nixon's staffers suggested leaning on the CIA during Watergate, even Richard Nixon blanched at this: 'You don't mess with Dick Helms,' he declared – on tape! Accused of having overthrown various Latin American governments, which he cagily refused to admit, he displayed his well-known ruthlessness when it came to line calls. He proved a demanding partner, chiding me for 'standing there like a potted plant' when, panting from exhaustion, I failed to retrieve some hopeless situation. Crack-of-dawn summonses to tennis with him always ended with the words 'Over and out.'

Meanwhile, despite the excruciating hours, my job had many positive aspects, such as being chosen to show Eric Clapton around the White House in a purple zoot suit (his, not mine), though I didn't really like his stubbly beard. There followed in his wake Jon 'Living on a Prayer' Bon Jovi, who was very cute but rather short. Showing admirable commitment, I still go to their concerts when they have them (I got into trouble at a Clapton concert in London by standing on my front-row seat during 'Layla' and yelling applause, until the disgruntled Brits behind me decided to stand up too and join in).

As I always volunteered for every errand there, I got to know the denizens of the West Wing pretty well. My favourite was the Secretary of State and former US Marine Jim Baker, who always managed to arrive from strange far-off places like Alma-Ata looking absolutely impeccable. With boundless energy and intelligence, when in danger of being thwarted a sort of gunfighter's look could be detected in his eyes. There wasn't much to criticise about his or the President's foreign policy anyway, which didn't stop the Democrat-leaning press from trying. They were herded very firmly by his press secretary, Margaret Tutwiler, also known as Queen Tut or Rottweiler, and as necessary by Baker himself. Any cheap shots were dealt with forthwith by him, with the offending correspondent banned from his plane. As few of the papers by this time had many of their own correspondents abroad and Baker was travelling at high velocity, it was near impossible to cover his exploits except from his aircraft.

Unfortunately, by this time, though both would (and did) deny it, there had been a really bad falling out between Baker and his hitherto closest friend, the President. When it came to Bush's choice of a vice-presidential candidate, the best choice would have been Baker, who had also served as Ronald Reagan's Treasury Secretary. But as both of them came from Texas, that was ruled out. To Baker's amazement, Bush announced the utterly unexpected choice of the very junior and inexperienced Dan Quayle, and a furious Baker was not even informed in advance. Assigning his friend Stu Spencer to mentor Quayle, Baker told Stu to 'let him hit the buffers a few times, then maybe he'll listen to you'. But Quayle kept hitting the buffers ever after.

It requires attempts at psychoanalysis to work out why the future President made this choice, which later was to be so costly for him. Having served very loyally but in a very subordinate role for eight years as Ronald Reagan's No. 2, it seemed that George Bush wanted to assert himself by choosing a deputy who was so clearly subordinate to him. This was unnecessary, as the Vice-President normally is so clearly subordinate anyway. But other explanations do not stack up. Quayle was from the Midwest, but there were better candidates from there. He was twenty years younger than Bush, but there were brighter luminaries his age, and a desirable characteristic of a Veep is supposed to be experience in case the President falls ill on his watch.

My other favourite was the national security

adviser, General Brent Scowcroft. An ultra-polite, ascetic workaholic, he was regarded by many as the best ever holder of the post. He was the President's right-hand man throughout the Gulf War but was not best pleased when, in his opinion, the President made the bad mistake of allowing the surrounded Iraqi tank forces to withdraw with their armour, which then was used to keep Saddam Hussein in power.

Brent, who typically arrived first at the White House and was the last to leave, was famous for always sleeping through Cabinet meetings, on the grounds that nothing of interest ever happened in them. The President, who had a Yale fraternity graduate sense of humour, would exploit this by suddenly talking very softly in Cabinet, then asking Brent for his opinion. Roars of laughter would then wake up the sleeping Brent, not one whit abashed. Years later I discovered, to my surprise, that Cabinet meetings are taken more seriously in the UK.

Among the other Cabinet members, Jack Kemp, former quarterback of the Los Angeles Rams, was, as he explained to me, the only senior figure in the administration who knew much about black America. This was because, as a quarterback, he had depended every week on the huge all-black members of the defensive line to save him from destruction at the hands of their opponents – and this had involved much congratulatory socialising with them. He did his best to improve things on the public housing estates, causing friction with the fearsome head of the Office of Management and Budget, Richard Darman. The Treasury Secretary, Nick Brady, launched the Brady bonds to help Latin America but did not get on with Congress, of which he held a low opinion.

The administration had its own splash of glamour in the wife of the Commerce Secretary, Georgette Mosbacher. She gave excellent parties, clad in barely-there dresses draped around her impressive frame. The Georgetown ladies pursed their lips, but she was understandably popular with the male half of the population.

By now, in the run-up to the Gulf War, I made an interesting discovery: the military, all of whom were Vietnam vets, were much less gung-ho about going to war than the civilians. They kept wanting to know not how a war was going to be started but how it was going to be ended. Reputedly among the peaceniks was the chairman of the joint chiefs of staff, General Colin Powell, who was always very nice to us peons whenever he surfaced at the White House.

Furthermore, a friend on the NSC staff who was a regular visitor to the Pentagon told me about the posters some mid-ranking figures had squirrelled away in their offices there. These were entitled 'What to do in the event of nuclear war'. The advice was to lower the blinds, move away from the windows to a corner of the room, adopt a crouching position with your head between your knees 'and kiss your ass goodbye!' I found this reassuring, as it seemed to demonstrate that this was an outcome they would prefer to avoid.

Meanwhile, none of us in the lower echelons really believed that we were heading for a war. We imagined there would be some kind of diplomatic outcome. But suddenly things changed and the atmosphere within the compound became electric.

The victory was swift too, and the President and Scowcroft made sure we did not chase Saddam to Baghdad and get bogged down in Iraq, as we did so unwisely under George W.

The President's approval ratings went through the roof, to around 80 per cent. Most of the Democrats had opposed the war and no one at this point believed that any of their potential candidates, the so-called 'seven dwarves', could seriously challenge Bush for re-election. Still the President was accused, including by some who had opposed the Gulf War, of failing to dispose of Saddam.

The President, when seeking election, had made his famous pledge: 'Read my lips: no new taxes.' But he had annoyed his conservative supporters by doing the opposite. This was a time when there was a lot of concern about the rapidly increasing national debt becoming a tax on future generations. A huge ticker tape display in Times Square showed New Yorkers how the debt was increasing at vertiginous speed by the day, the hour, the minute and the second. No one at the time had come up with the wheeze, employed by the Federal Reserve in

2008 and again more recently, of simply printing a trillion dollars or two to help us get by. The economy was struggling. The President kept arguing that the Federal Reserve Board should cut interest rates and Alan Greenspan later confessed that they should indeed have done so.

The Reaganites also were upset that, on being elected, the President had pledged 'a kinder, gentler America' ('Kinder than who?' asked Nancy Reagan), and even more by the fact that they had been pushed aside by the Bush political operatives taking over. Ronald Reagan's great strength had been his ability to communicate with blue-collar Americans. The Reaganites, now reduced to talking heads on TV, took to describing the Bush team as 'Country Club Republicans'! Stu Spencer, a key sidekick of Reagan in California, declared that George Bush knew more about Kuwait than California 'and maybe cared more about it too'. Barbara also was well known to dislike the glitzy atmosphere and inhabitants of Los Angeles.

In April 1992, five days of rioting and looting broke out in Los Angeles following the bizarre acquittal of four police officers filmed beating up Rodney King, a black American, and the shooting by a Korean storekeeper of a shoplifter. Every store in Koreatown was looted and torched, sixty-three people were killed and an army division had to be deployed to restore order. There followed, then as now, a failure even to begin to address the deep-seated problems afflicting sections of the black community on housing estates in the inner cities, which I saw at first-hand working for the United Way – the prevalence of single female or, in effect, no-parent families; of children growing up on the streets; of high rates of drug abuse and criminality. Without much more effective programmes to address these issues, getting rid of statues doesn't look likely to help very much. One current target, Andrew Jackson, was the founder of the Democratic Party and I was a bit surprised to find Black Lives Matter protesters in the UK defacing the statue of Abraham Lincoln. Perhaps they were aware, unlike most Brits, that he was a Republican.

Meanwhile, the electoral scene was seriously complicated by a bombastic, populist, egomaniac electronics billionaire from Texas, Ross Perot, running against the entire political establishment as an independent candidate for President. Although tiny, he spent a lot of money and made a lot of noise. A particular target of his was the North American Free Trade Agreement (NAFTA) championed by the President. Perot claimed that he could hear the 'giant sucking sound' of jobs being siphoned out of the US to south of the border. To be fair, he turned out to have had a point, as under NAFTA a host of American manufacturers shifted production to lower-cost sites in Mexico. Perot ended up winning 19 per cent of the votes in the election.

Back at the White House, hanging around there at this time was another of my former neighbours in Washington, usually to be found in dark glasses and clad in a bomber jacket. This was the President's eldest son, George W., who was part-owner and business manager of the Texas Rangers baseball team. No one could think of him as future presidential material at the time. The family themselves thought of his brother, Jeb, as their future political standard-bearer, and Jeb did become a successful

Governor of Florida before crashing in the presidential primaries against Donald Trump in 2016.

But George W. did have much shrewder political instincts than his father. He understood what was wrong with the White House, which in his view was the lack of cohesion, team spirit and even loyalty among many of the senior people there.

Soon to depart was the formidably efficient, intelligent and authoritarian chief of staff, John Sununu, bane of the environmentalists, against whom Sununu supported the Alaska oil pipeline. So did the President, who assured me that the caribou population up there loved it too, as it generated some heat, causing them to huddle against the pipeline in the winter. But featured in *Time* magazine as Bush's 'bad cop', the abrasive Sununu had made enemies inside as well as outside the building, and the press discovered that he had used official transport for private purposes on various occasions, including to visit his dentist in Boston. George W. felt that Sununu had become too unpopular and had let his father down.

Whatever its other problems, the White House of

George Herbert Walker Bush was determined to be squeaky clean on ethics – far more so than some of its successors. The best replacement would have been Baker, who would soon have restored some order, as the warring factions were all scared of him. But he was too busy reunifying Germany and managing the break-up of the Soviet Union.

So, to general amazement, the choice fell on the Transportation Secretary, Sam Skinner, who was indeed a much nicer guy but whose only apparent other qualification was that his wife, Honey, was a friend of Barbara. This was never going to work, and it didn't. The infighting continued, as did the incessant leaks. The President was far too nice a man to explode at these and investigate who was doing the leaking. For convenience's sake, the vehicle often employed was the *Washington Post*, which was bizarre, as hardly any of its readers were likely to vote Republican in any circumstances. The person who learned the most from this experience was George W., who, when he became President, enforced *omertà* and penalised those he considered too close to the press, including Colin Powell.

It was fascinating to see him, years later, as President, behaving as the polar opposite of his father. Far more politically savvy, better at domestic policy, more of a real Texan and far closer to his political base, Bush Junior launched some imaginative programmes such as 'No child left behind'. Being a graduate of the Harvard Business School did not prevent him from being portrayed as rather dim by the Democrat-leaning press, which was not the case at all. The problem was rather, to bowdlerise Donald Rumsfeld, that he didn't know what he didn't know – in particular about the Middle East. He believed that the US troops would be welcomed as liberators in Iraq, which for about fifteen minutes they were. His appointment of Rumsfeld as Defense Secretary was swallowed with great difficulty by George W.'s father, who had been a victim of Rumsfeld's plotting against him in the Ford administration. To my certain knowledge (though publicly both denied it), not only Brent Scowcroft but the President's father also tried to warn George W. against invading Iraq, with no success. He kept saying that Saddam had tried to assassinate his dad, which was

true, and he seemed to feel that he should complete
the job his father had failed to finish. He also gen-
uinely believed that Saddam had weapons of mass
destruction and was appalled when none were
found. Instead, in his terms at least, he vindicated
the Bush presidencies in a different way, by serving
two terms and not just one.

Meanwhile I had befriended another extremely tall, but mercifully not red-haired, more senior
and influential White House adviser. A favourite
of the President, he was prepared to waste his time
on me because I was reputed to be a much hum-
bler one myself. He confided his concerns about
a rival White House dignitary whom he regarded
as far more dangerous to the Republic than any of
the Soviets. Proving to be no less eccentric than
my previous suitor, his idea of a really good night
out was to invite me to his Georgetown mansion,
where we would sit at opposite ends of a dining
room table designed for twenty guests eating egg
salad prepared by the cleaning lady. As a result of
this cruel and inhuman treatment, and because
I was looking for an upgrade, at any rate in terms

of using my intelligence, I was bound to be sorely tempted when the Pizza King was appointed to the United States Embassy in a well-known European capital – on merit of course (he was a major donor to Republican Party coffers).

Loath to lose me as his tennis companion, my plan to move to The Hague was fiercely opposed by spymaster Richard Helms, on the grounds, he claimed, that 'nothing ever happens there'. He proved to be right about that, but I enjoyed the Netherlands and the Dutch and meeting their excellent Prime Minister, Ruud Lubbers.

As head of the ambassador's office, I had to be upgraded to Top Secret security clearance. This was so I could attend meetings in the bug-proof 'bubble', which included the deputy chief of mission, the military attaché and the CIA representative. As nearly always in US embassies, all the real work was done by the excellent deputy, a State Department career officer, leaving his boss as a figurehead at best. One of the ambassador's friends, who flew in from time to time, was a beautiful blonde who became a great friend of mine (I was and am a brunette) as we pursued our joint efforts to keep His Excellency out of trouble. To do so, my duties occasionally had to include accompanying him to the local black-tie casino, with a very helpful police escort. His contribution to international relations and greater understanding with the US was somewhat limited in the opinion of General Scowcroft, who excluded him from all meetings with the Dutch when the President came to visit.

One of his best friends was Roger Moore, with whom he used to exchange questionable faxes, but he was also on good terms with local royalty in the person of the leading local tycoon, who, unfortunately, had been kidnapped in his youth, with a ransom believed to have been paid for his release.

Meanwhile, we watched in dismay as my friend the President, who had succeeded so brilliantly in foreign policy, struggled domestically. Part of the problem had seemed obvious to someone even at my humble level. This was the glaring contrast between the quality of the President's foreign policy team and the utter mediocrity of his domestic political advisers. His head of domestic policy was a self-centred nonentity, taken seriously by nobody.

Nor was it even clear who was in charge of his re-election campaign. Nominally, this was Fred Malek, head of Marriott Hotels and now-defunct Northwest Airlines. Though always polite and very amiable, Malek seemed to lack both energy and ideas. For these, the President appeared to rely on his pollster, Robert Teeter, which was not a great success either.

But the problem, I and others feared, lay deeper than that. It was that George Bush Senior was not really a politician. A great public servant, he hated economics and wasn't really very interested in domestic policy. On becoming President, contrasting himself to Ronald Reagan, he had declared that he didn't really 'do the vision thing'. It was becoming obvious that he didn't really have one himself.

A crucial moment, and an opportunity to turn things around, came at Easter, when plans were gestated to persuade the President to replace Dan Quayle with a more credible candidate for the next

Vice-President, as the voters so clearly did not relish the prospect of Quayle taking over in any circumstances. If Bush had opted for Baker, irrespective of the Texas connection, he would have had a far better chance of being re-elected. Another possibility, canvassed at the time, was to promote Dick Cheney, who, whatever may be thought of his efforts when he *did* become Vice-President under George W., had performed very well as Defense Secretary in the Gulf War. There was even talk of Colin Powell.

Almost any other candidate would have helped. On a school visit, Quayle had been mercilessly mocked by the press for not knowing how to spell potato. Less forgivable was his habit of using the vice-presidential helicopter to fly, rather than drive, the few miles to the Congressional Club in Washington to play golf.

But Quayle by now was well aware of these manoeuvres. In a one-on-one meeting, he made an emotional appeal to the President not to dump him and, to the horror of his advisers, George Bush agreed to keep him on the slate. He did so in part,

I'm sure, because until almost the very last minute, he did not believe that the American people would reject him in favour of his far more questionable Democrat opponent. For apart from his evasion of military service, in which he was far from unique as a horde of well-connected young Americans had sought deferment, Bill Clinton had confessed pre-emptively, on TV, to having been unfaithful to Hillary.

The President's lack of vision seemed to be confirmed when Baker's brilliant deputy and future head of the World Bank, Bob Zoellick, was called in to draft a defining speech for the campaign. Asked what message he wanted to get across to the electorate, I heard the President's reply was that he would do a better job than the other guy.

Jim Baker, who wanted to continue as Secretary of State, did not enjoy being switched back – far too late – to the White House as chief of staff, and he became very pessimistic about the election.

By this time, two months before the 1992 election, I had returned to Washington to help with the campaign, receiving a warm welcome from 'your friend' the President, who remained confident that he would win. I had a few friends in the opposite camp and I knew what they were dreading – that in the TV debates the President would chide Clinton for dodging the draft and ask, 'What makes you think you are qualified to be commander in chief?' This would have been calculated to leave their candidate both flushed and flustered. But the President was too much of a gentleman ever to use this obvious tactic and the debates rolled on with Clinton talking glibly about the economy and the President, on one occasion, looking at his watch!

In November, I found that the better man had lost the election and with it I had lost my job. To be fair to the draft-dodger, when, years later, I met him at Le Caprice in London with a companion who bore no resemblance to Hillary, he was (of course) very charming, and I don't think he was a bad President. He was nothing if not a moderate; his adviser's famous theory of 'triangulation' really amounted to heading in whatever direction the wind was blowing.

When it came to Monica Lewinsky, it might

seem strange that my compatriots forgave him so easily for lying under oath. But the country was at peace, the economy was booming and forgive him they did.

A masterstroke of his was appointing Senator Lloyd Bentsen as his first Treasury Secretary. He had utterly crushed Dan Quayle in a TV debate, saying, 'I knew Jack Kennedy, and you are no Jack Kennedy.' More of an authentic Texan than the President, who generally seemed more Yale than Texas, when Bentsen wanted to leave a party, he was famous in Washington for throwing his wife over his shoulder before taking her home.

But will Bill Clinton really be remembered by many future historians?

Somehow, I don't think so. George H. W. Bush was a one-term President and, therefore, supposedly a failure. But history, so far, has not agreed. He left the White House close to tears, feeling that he had let his colleagues and his party down. But when he died, the tributes poured in from all over the world. For the world knew that it was very fortunate to have had him as President of the United

States during the invasion of Kuwait, the break-up of the Soviet Union and the reunification of Germany. He may not have been much of a politician. But he was something much rarer and more important than that: a true statesman. The headline I most loved about him read: 'HE WAS PROOF THAT A GOOD MAN CAN CHANGE THE WORLD'.

Leaving behind a broken-hearted European ambassador, who was, unfortunately, too short for me and whose car was too small for me even to get into (though he did send me poems almost every day), I had to trek back to Washington DC, with no prospect of any appointment by the new intern-chasing President. (No intern was ever allowed solo near the President or Oval Office on my watch!)

I sought refuge with Washington's grandest dame (not excluding the new First Lady), resuming my role as her tennis partner. I was pleased to have gotten rid of my tennis-pro suitor in Europe and to be reunited with the most important male in my life, a chocolate-coloured Labrador called Guinness, who used to surprise our guests by ringing the doorbell to get back into the house. He was extremely rude to anyone wanting to take me out, as he would plonk his backside in the front passenger seat of the car and refuse to allow anyone else to get in. I found this quite helpful from my point of view.

My hoity-toity former-White-House friends were now in the political wilderness for the next eight years but were as full of themselves as ever and blaming everyone else for this debacle. I was able to witness Georgetown playing its favourite game, which is to dump, as hastily as possible and without trace, all those they had courted so assiduously in the out-going administration, while fawning over the new arrivals.

I resumed my tennis matches with the legendary hostess at the Arlington YMCA, though she preferred to play outdoors in the summer. She informed me that she had found a tame diplomat with a tennis court that would be available on demand, but he was somewhat lacking in tennis skills.

I was saddled with this unfortunate while she played with the former White House counsel, who had a giant wingspan the size of a pterodactyl's. After watching my partner miss the first five volleys and barely get his service across the net, I informed him that each time the ball came our way I would shout 'mine' and if he would kindly get out of the way we could probably win the match. This worked pretty well, except that he continued to serve up numerous double faults, he claimed because he was distracted by the sight of me crouching beside the net. I told him firmly that this kind of behaviour might be OK in Europe but was frowned on in the United States.

One of my principal tennis adversaries was another European envoy, small but dynamic, who played all day, every day. His main weapon was psychological warfare. Walking onto the court with his opponent, he would ask, 'And how is your lousy backhand today?' He never tried this on me, as he knew to his cost that my backhand was awesome. On getting ready to serve, he would hoot, 'Ace warning!'; as his opponent readied himself to serve, he would shout, 'Fear is a terrible thing!' These tactics worked quite well in terrorising the diplomatic corps, but he proved not always able to cope with the approach I borrowed from Ivan Lendl of blasting returns straight through the man at the net. Also, he was on the short side for dealing with any overheads.

For a while, I joined the staff of a well-known political magazine, at which my main job was to be chased around my desk on a regular basis by an equally well-known political commentator. This was not a problem, as I was easily able to evade his sudden lunges. Naturally, he went on to become a senior adviser in the Clinton White House.

This job gave me the opportunity to watch at close quarters the political education of the Clintonites, as the new President's supporters and appointees descending on Washington were known at the time. Many of them had arrived there seeming to believe that they had a mandate to change the world. In fact, Bill Clinton had won the election with just 43 per cent of the votes. Many of the new arrivals, from Democrat-leaning think tanks and faculties, seemed alarmingly young. Before long, they were looking a lot older, as they found that wily and hard-boiled senators on both sides of the aisle were no pushovers.

The most brutal lesson of all was delivered to Hillary, who, to keep her happy, was empowered by the President to implement healthcare reform, but who had no legislative or other standing to do so. Presenting her ideas to the Senate, she was thrilled to be greeted with warm applause. But when her massive 1,000-page reform Bill reached the legislature, it was sunk without trace, not least because of a distressing lack of clarity as to how it was to be funded. She found herself obliged to retreat to largely ceremonial duties for the remainder of her husband's first term, before successfully making her own way in the Senate.

The outstanding feature of the new administration, though, was the quality of the economic team, led by Lloyd Bentsen as Treasury Secretary, who had more clout with Congress than any of his predecessors. Together with Alan Greenspan they persuaded Clinton to raise taxes to cut the deficit, which cost him dearly in the mid-term elections, but there was no doubting their competence.

4

AFTERLIFE

While these dramas were being played out, I was working on life after the White House. Having served there in the humblest possible position, but also as a friend of the President, how does one get over having been so near to the centre and having witnessed great events?

The answer, most often, is to get out of Washington, for it remains a company town with limited satisfaction for anyone not involved in government. A few of my friends remained, as talking heads filling space on the innumerable TV channels, and one or two became lobbyists, but they were now in subordinate roles.

Not only that, most people's lives are not centred around politics and nor is the profession particularly admired. So, I took the first and easiest step to get out, which was to head for California, *en route* to New York.

I bet you didn't know that, hidden away in the Russell Senate Building, there is a secret tennis court, paid for by the US taxpayer (unbeknownst to them) and frequented by sporty legislators, such as John Breaux and Dan Coats (the latter also from Indiana). Their tennis buddy was the former pro John Gardiner, who, during the recesses, would invite them to one of his camps.

My favourite tennis coach was the legendary Rick, head pro at the John Gardiner Tennis Ranch at a magical place in the Carmel Valley. He did not have much to work with in terms of clientele – Rupert Murdoch, Al Haig, Alan Greenspan, plus the owner of the legendary King Ranch in Texas and the former head of GE (before Jack Welch), who ran off with the gardener. There was also the head of Citicorp, who informed us that the days of nation states were numbered. Before long, he said, the world would be governed by a committee of international bankers. (This was before many of the said bankers combined in their effort to bankrupt us all.)

Rick believed in teaching with the aid of a certain amount of irony and even more sarcasm, accompanied by brutal imitations of his clients in action. A career in the US Navy appeared to have hardened his soul, but I was prepared to put up with his barbs in return for an amazing lunch beforehand, consisting of non-stop artichokes, avocados (from the neighbouring World Garlic Capital) and every other fruit and vegetable I could think of. While poor suckers down the valley in Carmel had to put up with fog until noon every day, the sun always shone on the valley at Gardiner's.

Once, when I asked Alan Greenspan about his game, he informed me that he had just won a set against his coach (definitely not Rick, who would have died rather than give any of us a single point). There were many similar acts or claims of bravado, with Rupert Murdoch concentrating on his boxing prowess, though without an opponent. By far the most dynamic and enthusiastic tennis player was Al 'I'm in charge' Haig, who raced around the court interfering with balls that clearly were his partner's, while Mrs Haig looked on tolerantly.

Just down the road at the Highland Lodge, I encountered a disillusioned pianist whose best years appeared to be behind him. I was assured that he could deliver a knock-out performance of 'Great Balls of Fire' but had not done so for several years. It took a skimpy Léger dress and a fair amount of alcohol to persuade him to perform.

Down the coast, at the Ventana Inn, as I munched my salad in the mist, I was horrified to hear the roar of what sounded like 1,000 motorbikes and be surrounded by leather-clad figures all wearing ponytails. It took a little while to figure out that the ponytails were all grey and this clearly was a Harley-Davidson convention for Bay Area retirees.

Moving on to Pebble Beach, I was able to observe overweight US business executives engaging in their favourite sport, which consisted of driving around the gorgeous seaside golf course in their carts, with only the occasional need to strike a ball. This would inevitably be followed by sundowner drinks before the sun had even begun to think about setting.

5

ADVENTURES IN
MANHATTAN

I had concluded that maybe the moment had arrived for me to try out my skills in Manhattan. This was at the time when, in *Slaves of New York*, Tama Janowitz explained that finding an apartment in New York was so expensive and near impossible that most ladies of her acquaintance ended up having to cohabit with unsuitable partners simply in order to find a place to live. I chose instead to rent an apartment on Park Avenue South near Union Square, which I definitely could *not* afford, as it cost rather more than I could expect to be paid. The apartment was really small but appealing, and the doormen rescued me on many occasions over the next two years. The main disadvantage was the garbage trucks that came round at 4 a.m. each day, revenging themselves on those of us on the lower floors by sounding like volcanoes erupting as they emptied the bins. Plus, in the Mayor Dinkins era, there was the occasional sound of gunshots.

My first task was to help an immensely distinguished former United States ambassador to persuade a bunch of US corporations to contribute to a foundation fund to celebrate the fiftieth anniversary of the United Nations. I threw myself whole-heartedly into this fulfilling task and, thanks to the ambassador, we got in to see the CEOs of most of the leading companies in the United States, including Coca-Cola, Xerox and IBM, all of whom listened politely to our pitch before informing us that, in their opinion, the United Nations should be resolutely abolished, the headquarters on the East River should be turned into condos and the no-good diplomats hanging out in New York City should be required to pay their parking tickets on pain of death.

While working late on the UN account, I suffered a chastening New York experience. Staying overnight at the UN Plaza hotel, I switched on the TV, only to discover that the previous inhabitant had accessed a porn channel. As I struggled with the control to change this, to my horror, I heard knocks on the window and found a couple of window cleaners laughing and giving me thumbs-up signs, *though my room was on the 41st floor!* I had to roll across the bed and try to hide beneath it for a while.

I had, meanwhile, been introduced to a well-known private equity entrepreneur who, I was assured, would look after me in the Big Apple (despite his attempted flirtation with a well-known princess at the time). He also was reputed to be a formidable tennis player. The introduction turned out to be a not unqualified success as, after an hour's tussle, he limped off the court claiming to have torn one or both hamstrings and wanted resuscitation – which I declined.

By this time one of my business acquaintances had become over-enthusiastic about me. I suffered six months of siege tactics from which I was saved only by the huge, plucky doorman of my apartment and my equally large and gutsy black female assistant.

This was a stressful time for me, and as a result my former tennis partner from Washington was able to make inroads to which otherwise he would not have been able to aspire. He would turn up at weekends with flowers from the Korean grocer around the corner and very shrewdly befriended and bribed the doormen to keep my boss out and let him into my building. Knowing that I normally only eat lettuce, carrots and occasionally nuts, he would lure me to the Union Square Café for a macrobiotic lunch, even though I never usually *do* lunch. He turned out to be surprisingly keen on scooting around the dance floor at the Rainbow Room and proved fearless in taking me to the lamented Au Bar and other dives. At one of these, we inadvertently gatecrashed the birthday party of

Lennox Lewis, at the time heavyweight champion of the world, getting a very friendly reception.

On a visit to Denver, we played tennis in a howling gale on the roof of a hotel, resulting in a first-ever victory for him as I found it difficult to simultaneously hold down my tennis skirt, throw up the ball and whack a serve (try it sometime, believe me). I was dragged off to a pseudo-corral called the Grizzly Rose, where the line-dancing advertising executives, all dressed in their cowboy outfits, were surprised to be treated to a lightning-fast foxtrot through the middle of their line! I was mortified, but my partner chose to ignore the horrified expressions of the dedicated line dancers in their cowboy boots and hats. I closed my eyes and tried to pretend I wasn't there.

Although I had become popular in my PR company, especially with the eighty-year-old founder, as the UN account had not found favour with any donors it was thought best for me to try my hand at advertising. I moved sideways to grand offices on Madison Avenue. My colleagues consisted of fiendishly talented New Yorkers who had barely even heard of the Midwest and certainly had no intention of ever going to any of the 'fly-over' states as they commuted to and from Los Angeles.

In an effort to keep up with these uber-nerds, I would get dressed up each morning in my multi-coloured Barami suits with short skirts and padded shoulders. As I emerged from the lift one day, towering over a male colleague in my stilettos, he inquired, 'Where do you come from? Not this planet, I presume?'

After this successful coup, I was put in charge of – guess what? The pregnancy test account, of course – Clearblue Easy! I struggled to make much impact with this, so was told to help save the US Postal Service, which was and is under dire threat from emails, FedEx, DHL and worse.

This was at a time when, under Mayor Dinkins, New York was bidding to become the crime capital of the world. Commuters from New Jersey, queuing in their cars to reach the city through the Lincoln Tunnel, were subjected to harassment by the famous squeegee bandits. They would offer to clean the windows of your car, while threatening reprisals by way of broken windscreens if the offer was declined. Many corners of mid- and uptown Manhattan seemed to be infested by groups of youths, loitering for no obvious purpose. Anyone venturing into Central Park after dark was taking his or her life into their hands. Leaving my swanky office on Madison Avenue at 7.30 one evening, I was dragged into an alley, mugged at gunpoint and beaten up by two members of the minority community, with no one interfering in the struggle. Of course, this couldn't last, and it didn't. Rudy Giuliani became mayor on a law-and-order ticket. With a new police chief, they pursued a zero-tolerance policy. The squeegee bandits disappeared from the Lincoln Tunnel, as did the groups of youths loitering on street corners.

Today, my friends there tell me, things seem to have come round full circle, with the present mayor infuriating Governor Cuomo (who ought to have been, but wasn't, the Democratic candidate in the 2020 presidential election) by failing to prevent some spectacular looting and cutting the police budget by $1 billion. In the words of America's most famous philosopher: 'It's déjà vu all over again.' (Other favourite Yogi Berra-isms are, of course, 'No one goes there any more; it's too crowded' and, more alarmingly, 'The future ain't what it used to be.')

My hospitalisation following the attack was brief, but the episode did render more appealing the prospect of migrating from New York.

6

HOW TO BE
AN ALIEN

Invited to re-cross the Atlantic, the main reason I agreed to do so was to bring me closer to my long-standing idol, Sting. In my teens, I never missed a Police concert anywhere within striking range in the US. This was in the days of occasional fist fights on stage between Sting and Stewart Copeland, as they competed for primacy in the band. I know every single Police song from 'Don't Stand So Close to Me' to 'Every Little Thing She

Does Is Magic' and sing along shamelessly – some would say tunelessly – whenever I get the chance.

I hopefully assumed that Sting would be both accessible and not impervious to my charms, but I discovered to my distress that Trudie keeps him on a very short leash. I had a very near miss one evening at the swanky Nobu eatery on Park Lane, only for the head waiter to throw himself into a protective position in front of Sting in the nick of time. I have not, however, given up my quest and recently had another near miss in Juan-les-Pins. I cruised past his hotel in my Morgan, but he may have been distracted by the presence on the Riviera of fifteen ladies from the Crazy Horse in Paris. Next, I tracked him down in Cannes, but my noisy encouragement at his concert there was not successful either, except with his partner 'It Wasn't Me' Shaggy, who did seem well disposed.

I really like the Brits, despite their damp and foggy island. But I knew that some of them could be very snooty about culture, so I had to figure out how on earth to acquire some above and beyond what I had absorbed in Muncie and Michigan. Checking with my local contacts how I could become civilised within six months and able to hold my own re. culture with the locals, I was advised to enrol at Christie's art school and study hard in the course there. I learned to distinguish between a Sisley and a Pissarro, not to mention a Boucher and a Fragonard. The only real competition came from a cute English blonde who was so irritatingly knowledgeable that I could not resist one morning giving her a friendly Midwestern kick in the butt! Although a bit surprised by this, she reacted positively, and we became firm friends. An attempt to become civilised in another manner by enrolling in a cordon bleu course was less successful, as I lasted just one day.

On arriving in London, I was befriended by a decidedly eccentric old peer of the realm, who was famous for appearing at the House of Lords and elsewhere with a parrot on his shoulder. The Brits proved surprisingly accessible. Prince Charles may talk to trees, but he was very nice to me at lunch

– which normally I abhor ('Lunch is for wimps' – Gordon Gekko) – and so was a charming, relaxed and *fun* John Major.

I was abducted one weekend to the Isle of Wight, where some sort of regatta the locals take seriously was underway. Needless to say, I was invited to crew on the Richard Branson boat but then was made to pay for some Pimm's-induced boasting about my prowess at golf, which led to well-merited embarrassment as I swung and missed on the first tee.

Another embarrassment arose at Annabel's, where I had squeezed myself into a full-length gown which, regrettably, proceeded to split down the middle as I sat down to dine. Camouflage was urgently required by the maître d' to retrieve my dignity, forging an enduring bond between me and the Mark Birley staff (now sadly dispersed).

I discovered that the Brits do not always know my native country quite as well as they think they do. An early acquaintance (of course) was Peter Mandelson, whom I really like as he is always nice to me, and I sometimes bump into him in unexpected places e.g. the Bahamas. Re-introduced to him at a swanky London party as a Trump supporter (as, naturally, I did vote for the Republican candidate for President), he confided that he had never met one before! I rest my case.

• • •

By this time, for reasons I still cannot explain, I had developed a weakness for my transatlantic tennis-playing companion, leading to the sudden appearance of our son, Alexander. His debut in the world was controversial, as when I attempted to get him christened in front of a large congregation, he put up a fight of which Cassius Clay would have been proud, accompanied by yowling that could be heard all over SW1. It required a hefty contribution to church funds to get them to deliver a certifi-cate that he had, after all, become a fully paid-up member of the Church of England (episcopalian to me).

I took very seriously my new responsibilities as a future school mom, particularly as my other half was somewhat lacking in parenting skills. He would disappear for most of the week but then reappear to take our son, aged two, to the chocolate shop across the road, on one occasion doing so amidst a snowstorm in mid-February with the infant not wearing any shoes. When the lady in the shop kindly pointed this out, he expressed surprise that the child had not warned him of his shoeless status. I could give other examples of his deficiencies in this respect. Ever since, parenting, by joint agreement, has been left to me.

In the role of a school mom, for which I am not ideally cut out, I had to watch in freezing rain as my beloved child was trodden underfoot by a bunch of hooligans playing a peculiar version of American football without the padding. I was, however, converted to an ardent supporter of Jonny Wilkinson (cute) and Martin Johnson (threatening) for the very good reason that they hardly ever lost. At Twickenham, I learned to sing 'Land of Hope and Glory' and 'Jerusalem' but could not for the life of me understand what 'Swing Low, Sweet Chariot' has got to do with England or rugby.

In the summer, I can be found on the tennis courts at Queen's or having lunch with Novak Djokovic (so far only once!). Since it's near impossible for members to play during the pre-Wimbledon tournament there, I sit doggedly under my umbrella in the rain with a very big smile for the TV cameras. High points have included witnessing John McEnroe indignantly denying he was John McEnroe to a member seeking his autograph.

My other half, before I even met him, fell in love with South Africa – not with the politics, which are often dire, but because, he contends, 'it's a magnificent country'. So every year in the fall, with my offspring, I was lured into the African bush with ace ranger Piet to see buffaloes charging lions, and an angry hippo throwing a bushbuck that had sought refuge in its waterhole to a pack of wild dogs. Realising it had behaved really badly, the hippo tried to hide behind a small bush; unsuccessfully, as 4 million people by now have seen the video of this crime. No less magnificent is the Cape seen from the estate of Simon van der Stel, first governor of the province, surrounded by the beautiful gardens created by Sandy and Andrew Ovenstone.

The much sought-after school in which my kid was enrolled seemed to need both livening up and a more dedicated burst of fundraising than scones and tea. With a few exceptions, the Brits don't really *do* fundraising, preferring instead to rely on the welfare state, so I had to get together with my mainly US buddies to show them how to shoot the lights out fundraising-wise. Thanks to Lloyd Dorfman and the parents, we managed to raise a load of money for scholarships. Apart from falling off the stage in another full-length dress (during a live auction at the Mercers' Hall), this was an un-qualified success. I have had offers to become, if not the face, at any rate the bottom of Hérve Léger, of which I have amassed an impressive collection.

My attempts to disguise myself as a Brit by this time were being helped by my friend and neigh-bour, ace milliner Philip Treacy. Beneath one of his hats I could always look the part, though I am not the Ascot type (preferring the Kentucky Derby).

By this stage, I had been persuaded to apply for

a British passport – without, of course, giving up my American one. At the swearing-in ceremony, I was upstaged by a young lady from Belarus, who celebrated her new citizenship by wrapping herself around the presiding officer. He didn't seem to mind, and I hope they are now living happily ever after.

Confronted, as I frequently am, with ladies whose chests are slightly more provocative than my own, I headed for St John's Wood to check out the options available. The surgeon suggested some improvement but reassured me by saying if he bumped into me on a Saturday night he would thank his lucky stars. I was so touched by this that I failed to think of reporting him to the British Medical Association.

My earliest experiences of the London dining scene were at the Brasserie at Brompton Cross in the days when Imran Khan frequented it, before he discovered religion. When I protested to the very Gallic waiter about the slug crawling across my Caesar salad, he stared at me accusingly as if I had put it there, and insisted on including the salad and the slug in the bill.

Things took a turn for the better at Le Caprice, where I made an unfortunate debut by leaning towards my companion across a lighted candle, thereby setting my liberally hair-sprayed hair on fire, resulting in the near-evacuation of the restaurant. However, this dramatic incident succeeded in drawing me to the attention of the moving spirit there, the legendary Jesus Adorno.

Other notable experiences included the lamented Canteen in Chelsea Harbour, frequented by Tom Jones and owner Michael Caine, which had a tarte tatin the equal of anything in France. And one memorable evening at La Famiglia, we dined alone as the waiters, sensibly ignoring us, gathered around an ancient TV to watch Italy play Brazil in the final of the World Cup in Los Angeles. This event was supposed to popularise soccer in the United States but fell a bit short, as after 120 minutes of unspeakable boredom no goal had yet been scored. By this time, the entire TV audience in the USA had passed out unconscious. Brazil eventually won on penalties, causing the Italian head waiter to tell me that he no longer had anything left to live for.

Since then, our entire neighbourhood has been taken over by a gentleman from Sardinia called Mauro. Having arrived in London as a penniless waiter, he has managed by now to surround us with the pizzeria around the corner, frequented by Madonna in heavy disguise, a fish restaurant two blocks away, a meat restaurant outside our back door, a delicatessen and an Olivo, where I had a couple of disagreements with the legendary 007, now sadly deceased. Having failed to put in my contact lenses, I found my neighbour coughing in an exaggerated fashion and trying to swat the fumes of my illicit cigarette away with his napkin. This seemed to me inappropriately squeamish be-haviour for someone with a licence to kill and, once it dawned on me who he was, I did not hesitate to tell him so. Soon after, he withdrew into tax exile in the Bahamas, which he found a good base from which to campaign for Scottish independence. But I had to admit he had a point. Now down to one or at most two strictly private puffs a week, I can claim that it was James Bond who made me (virtually) give up smoking.

In pursuit of my goal never again to be found with a single surplus kilo, no gym or health club in central London has proved safe from me. At the Peak, towards the end of the day, I can be seen doing my (at least) seventy laps per day, leaving the offspring of Arab royalty panting in my wake. They make feeble efforts to catch up or to intercept me but are usually unable to get anywhere close. Other regulars include Matt Damon and Renée Zellweger training for their movies, as well as the James Bond villainess Grace Jones, who turned out to be surprisingly friendly.

Having previously been told that I needed to improve my daytime attire, which consists entirely of sneakers and gym clothes, I decided to invest in an Elizabeth Hurley denim skirt, admittedly on the short side and also full of (intentional) holes. While raising few, if any, eyebrows in London, on holiday in America this caused a split vote of the membership committee in the Leland Country Club, when the gentlemen members voted in my favour and the elderly ladies voted to keep me out! The skirt had to be shelved for a few years to ensure my admittance, but I am now thinking of reactivating it.

In London and elsewhere, from time to time I am intercepted in the swimming pool, gym or tennis court by would-be well-wishers who seek to engage me in conversation and arrange joint social activity. My other half does not *do* social activity, of which he claims to have had an overdose. He is by nature grumpy anyway and only relents if confronted by attractive ladies in skimpy outfits. Unfortunately, he receives effective back-up from my offspring, who in such situations keeps grabbing me and hissing, 'Come on, Mom.' All this is severely curtailing my social life, as I have not yet figured out a way to escape their clutches.

Excessive sports and non-stop jogging have left me with a first-class knowledge of the London medical community. One famous transgender surgeon used a large red marker pen to write her initials on my backside to indicate which hip she would 'resurface' first.

When it came to my next tennis injury, I developed a weakness for a very uptight British professor, kissing him repeatedly when he tried to escape my advances. Having fixed my knee, he refused to see me for the next six months, telling me that I needed to give my medical advisers a well-deserved holiday by going out to pasture with a bale of hay!

As I am now partly cobalt/chrome, no airport scanner fails to go off when I am around and my other half claims that he now personally owns up to 20 per cent of my body parts.

7

FOOTNOTES FROM THE MEDITERRANEAN

As part of my transatlantic acclimatisation, and to escape the blowy beaches and freezing water of the Hamptons, I have picked up the European habit of heading in the summer for the south of France. This does require an attempt at any rate to try to look as good as some of the locals, which is quite a challenge as some of them look very good indeed. I have in fact been a cover girl, but only in South Korea(!), some plucky Asiatic photographers having intercepted me on a safari in the African bush with my favourite ranger, Piet. People seem surprised to discover that I also have a brain, even though my spelling remains deficient, requiring frequent corrections by my laptop.

Writing this, I am installed on the terrace of the most beautiful restaurant in the Mediterranean, looking out over numerous yachts on the deep blue sea, though I think it may be smaller than the Great Lakes back where I come from. I am wearing my kick-ass Louboutin boat shoes with red soles and silver studs and my turquoise sequinned cowboy hat. Someone has to give all the passing Natashas in their skimpy outfits and sky-high heels some competition.

One of my favourites here is the aristocratic head doorman. He is famous for having broken up a bibulous scuffle between France's best-known actor and an even better-known one from the US with the words 'Behave yourselves, gentlemen!'

To my surprise, I am on friendly terms with the leading Russian gangster in the south of France. Although, according to his bestselling (in Russia) memoirs, he polished off a sadistic prison warder and ran the protection racket for GUM, the Moscow version of Harrods, he always greets me with a cry of 'Bravo!' He is popular in these parts for having helped to rescue four French hostages from Chechnya in exchange for one of the rebel Chechen leaders. The French were stuck as the Siberian prison governor contended that the Chechen was too dangerous to be released alive. The solution was to wait until another prisoner died, then to switch the identities so the Chechen could be released deceased.

My new friend keeps asking me what he can do for me, though he assures me that he is now retired. I don't think he can be very homesick here as the menus are in Russian and the bay is full of over-sized boats owned by his compatriots.

Another acquaintance is an Asian oligarch who has a tendency to wear white satin outfits and drive around in a purple four-by-four with matching bodyguards in tow. He appears at the tennis court with the captain of his yacht carrying his tennis rackets but is not very reliable with the line calls.

I keep meaning to come here for the film festival, but the locals tell me that invariably it rains for the whole two weeks and all the films are headache-inducing arthouse movies which no one has ever been known to see once they have won the prize. The only fun ever has been the occasional wardrobe malfunction affecting scantily clad French actresses on the red carpet. But even that has been offset by their determination to give us all long lectures about politics and life in general when receiving their misallocated prizes. The French, good for them, refuse to take this lying down, greeting these tirades with a chorus of hisses and boos.

Some people reckon that the French can be very patronising and snooty, but I find that if you wear very high heels and a cowboy hat, they can be very friendly and respond well to kisses on the cheek and broken French.

I am on friendly terms with the best-known Riviera bombshell, a famously well-constructed Swedish blonde who is sky high even without her heels, leaving most of the population gazing up at her in awe. She organises the pit girls for the

Formula One races through the narrow streets of Monaco. When it was proposed to banish the pit girls on supposedly anti-sexist grounds, the drivers threatened a strike. No one who has witnessed Lewis Hamilton careering past the Hotel de Paris at 290km per hour, screaming to the pits about the state of his tyres with 'Mad Max' Verstappen trying to shunt him out of the way, could possibly begrudge them their pit girls.

Another regular visitor to these parts, with whom I have had some encounters when swimming, is a famous French writer, well known for wearing his shirt open to the navel and married to a super-attractive actress. He has written some good books, but according to Hillary Clinton he helped to persuade her to bomb Libya, which turned out not to have been such a good idea. He bumps into me on a regular basis by swimming backwards in the pool, waving his arms amidst sudden changes of direction, and frequently zagging across me prior to asking me for a drink as I climb disgusted out of the pool.

My entire regime depends on a rapid seventy laps

swum at full tilt at the end of the day with the aid of huge flippers and webbed gloves. Anyone with any sense can see me coming and quickly get out of the pool, as there have been many casualties.

My favourite, and by far the most intelligent, of my friends here is a world-class backgammon and cards player, who is reputed to have transferred half the proceeds of oil sales in the Middle East back, via Aspinalls and other London gambling establishments, into safe Western hands. Able to calculate the odds with the speed of a super-fast computer, he excels by taking most of the luck out of the so-called games of chance. I would count on him to calculate the odds to the nth degree every single time – without any interference from a single dry martini while doing so. When I suggested we should have a friendly game of cards, he expressed horror at the thought. 'I don't play for fun, I only play seriously,' he roared. When I have asked others about his reputed success in his chosen profession, the response has been a shudder of horror at the thought of sitting down at any table with him. His life must have been mainly nocturnal for many years, but these days he can be found with his beautiful wife and daughter floating offshore on his yacht in the daytime too.

Also to be found roaming around is an extremely well-known American actor who insists on masquerading under the name of Monsieur Berger. This disguise is easily penetrated as he scarcely speaks a word of French. *Bonjour M. Berger*, I say to him cheerfully but without much success as, notoriously, he is only interested in dusky ladies.

There is also a very interesting English actress who can look really glamorous or like an ill-dressed tramp according to the time of day. She once very shrewdly asked if my son was naughty. 'He has a naughty look,' she observed. I had to admit that he was still a work in progress.

Right now, I am in disguise under an enormous Mexican straw hat. But my occasional tennis partner, Gaby, claims that she can recognise me by my derrière. She then upstaged me by inviting me to visit her yacht. When I asked how to find it, she said that if I turned right in the yacht harbour, I would find it right next to a large French yacht called *Desirée*. Arriving in an uber-chic Mini, the only boat we could find next to *Desirée* was an ocean liner built mainly of antique mahogany. This turned out to be Gaby's palace for the summer, though it is rented out in the winter to the British monarch and other members of the family when the Public Accounts Committee isn't looking.

Meanwhile, I am having problems with my tennis coach. He is a huge, friendly bear of a Frenchman who used to be champion in Monaco, defeating all other players in the principality. I am very fond of him, though he has some strange habits. One day, as an attractive blonde walked past the court, he put down his racket and started howling like a wolf, ignoring my remonstrances.

Playing down the road at the beautiful Monte Carlo Country Club has its challenges, as my for some reason favourite pro there tries to prevent me winning a single point, while congratulating himself noisily ('Bravo, Patrick!') whenever he hits the ball past me. The one consolation is that I have established friendly workout relations with Rafa, who, when others are chased out of the gym, kindly agrees to let me stay!

Despite my erstwhile successes in the Midwest, to my horror, on a recent stay in Portugal, the very dishy tennis coach, Miguel, said how nice it was that my son didn't mind playing with family members who were not quite up to his standard! I was incandescent with rage at this, threatening to cut off his ponytail. The situation was saved by the Brazilian guitarist, Perceval, who kept playing 'The Girl from Ipanema' for me. I have always felt a good deal of sympathy for this lady who, tanned and gorgeous, went down every day to the beach gazing straight past or through adoring males.

The other notable local feature is Gigi's super-chic shack on the beach, with the world's freshest fish still twitching as it is fried or baked. Not only that, Gigi is an opera fan, so you are deafened by Maria Callas, Pavarotti and the three tenors as you devour your fish! Apart from opening the champagne with his cutlass, whenever he sees arriving a female guest he approves of, he rings an old brass ship bell.

On a foray into Cannes, I am sitting by the
Mediterranean again next to Uma Thurman and
Quentin Tarantino. The Brit claims that I look
(almost) as good as Thurman – clearly in the
hope that I will do his bidding for the rest of the
day. Uma has been making clear that she is in full
single-mother, down-to-earth, anti-glamour mode
(cigarette, hamburger, fries and full-fat Coke).
Good for her! Tarantino has been holding forth
on the fate of gay marines at the end of the Second
World War. We have to hope this isn't going to be
the subject of his next movie.

And of course I encountered Harvey Weinstein.
I was a bit miffed that he did not invite me, like
so many others, to his room to watch him shower,
denying me the opportunity to turn down so unat-
tractive a prospect.

Today I nearly managed to mess up an expensive
perfume shoot with Natalie Portman, who, by the
way, looks every bit as good in the flesh as she does
on the screen, and a large black-tie-clad crowd by
mingling with them in my iridescent lime-green

The appearance
of Alexander.
Author's collection

Introducing Alex to President George W. Bush. Author's collection

Getting dressed up for fundraising at Mercers' Hall. Author's collection

My favourite males.

Author's collection

Imagining I am
in the Oval Office.

© Loic Bisoli

Trying to look glamorous. © Loic Bisoli

In Cannes and Antibes. © Loic Bisoli

Joie de vivre. © Loic Bisoli

On the Riviera. © Loic Bisoli

With Morgan. Author's collection

At Eden Roc. © Loic Bisoli

My favourite Brit.

Author's collection

tennis attire until they succeeded in shooing me away. In my quest to try to look as good as the French, a secret weapon has been the photographer Loic Bisoli, who helped with the pictures in the plate section of this book.

8

BUT WHAT ABOUT NOW?

*R*IP *well-loved Washington Redskins.* In a great leap forward for political correctness, they have been obliged to change their name. Quite how this will help American Indians, I haven't yet worked out.

I lived and worked in Washington at a better time. The US has just experienced a bizarre election between two candidates controversial within their own parties. The polls and mainstream media promised a Democrat 'blue wave', giving them control of the White House and both houses of Congress and enabling them to pursue their plans for $4 trillion-worth of tax increases and several trillions more in spending. Instead, the election restored my faith in the checks and balances in our constitution and the strength of our democracy.

The Bush Republicans were never reconciled to Donald Trump. Neither President Bush voted for him in 2016. George W. Bush did not campaign for Trump on this occasion either. They were disgusted by his treatment of Jeb Bush and deplored his apparent inability to ever sound presidential. Tax cuts and deregulation stimulated the economy, but when it came to dealing with coronavirus, in his concern to keep the economy open, he quarrelled with his scientific advisers and advertised to the end his hostility to face masks, ending up contracting the virus himself. Melania Trump, who always wore a mask, was astonished to find staffers and Congressional visitors wandering around the White House without them. 'What's wrong with these people?' she enquired. Good for her!

But, once again, Trump proved a formidable

campaigner, confounding the media and the polls because a lot of blue-collar and other ordinary Americans felt that he had tried to do more for them than Obama/Biden, and was more akin to their way of thinking about America too. A female presenter on CNN was unable to understand why he was winning so many votes because 'he is so unpopular' – she was convinced! But he failed to appeal to the swing voters who decide elections. He will go on trying to blame his defeat on electoral fraud. He was never likely to be a good loser.

Largely unnoticed has been the fact that the Republicans in Congress polled *better* than Trump. Not a single Republican Congressman lost his seat. Moderate Democrats blamed their losses on the left-wing 'Squad', detested by the Democratic Speaker Nancy Pelosi, talking about socialism and de-funding the police.

So what now can be expected from Joe Biden as President? For over forty years in the Senate he represented neighbouring Delaware, causing one opponent to describe him as the 'Loch Ness monster of the Washington swamp'! A survivor of horrendous personal tragedies (the deaths of his first wife, his daughter and his eldest son), the most important quality about him is his likeability, which I experienced on Capitol Hill and again in a brief encounter more recently. He seeks to be someone who is easy to get on with, which helped to get him chosen as Vice-President by Barack Obama.

He has made some spectacular mistakes. He voted against the war to liberate Kuwait but for the invasion of Iraq. In the meeting that decided on the raid that killed bin Laden, his advice was 'Don't go!'

In the Democratic primary contest, he was struggling against the left-wing candidates Elizabeth Warren and Bernie Sanders. But neither had the support of the black community. Biden did, and the polls kept showing that only the perceived moderate and 'regular guy' Biden could defeat Trump, though he had to promise his own supporters that he would be 'the most progressive President in US history'.

The Covid-19 pandemic increased his chances by

enabling him for months to run a largely subterranean campaign from his home in Delaware – the so-called 'basement strategy'. Avoiding discussion of his party's 'tax and spend' economic programme, he was counting on Donald Trump to defeat himself. But, crucially, where Biden did succeed was in presenting himself as a unifier, not a divider. This was the winning card for him, more so than his party's policy agenda.

He will be a far more normal President than Trump, with voters being offered a quieter life. He has promised an end to the daily barrage of tweets. He may not find the struggle against coronavirus much easier than Trump did, but there will be vaccines and no quarrels with his scientific advisers. He wants the US to join the Climate Change Convention and host a world climate summit (we have in fact meanwhile been decreasing our emissions, while others have been increasing theirs). He will try to avoid tariff wars and to restart nuclear discussions with Iran. There will be no more strident challenging of the status quo and a sigh of relief has gone around Europe, though not among the US allies in the Middle East, with whom Trump was popular for standing up to their sworn enemy, Iran.

But Biden will have to take account of the way Trump has changed some of the rules of the game. Globalisation has proved a bad experience for many blue-collar Americans, with massive job losses and US corporations transferring production to Mexico and Asia. Biden, who is close to the trade unions, claims to be as committed as Trump to 'bringing American jobs back home'. Trump was the only Western leader prepared to seriously challenge China over industrial espionage and blatantly one-sided trade relations, though others since have followed in his wake.

Trump was far more cautious about the use of force than his former adviser John Bolton, who wanted military action against Iran and North Korea and in Venezuela! But he, or rather General Mattis, did largely dispose of the Islamic State. Unlike the Nobel Peace Prize winner Obama, Trump took action against the Syrian regime for the use of chemical weapons and responded to Iranian military provocations by killing their chief organiser, General Soleimani. Biden will be just as cautious as Obama about getting involved in any conflict. Our days of policing the world are over (thank goodness).

Bill Clinton was elected, then re-elected, because he showed that he would stand up to the left wing of his party. That was what his 'New Democrats' (well before 'New Labour') were all about. In response to a wave of violent crime in US cities in 1994, Biden, on behalf of Clinton, pushed through the Senate a tough anti-crime bill, including 'stop and search' and the building of a lot more prisons, for which he has been apologising ever since as it led to the imprisonment of more young black Americans.

His running mate, the senator from California Kamala Harris, was selected as a 'woman of colour'. Her father was from Jamaica and her mother an immigrant from India. She was chosen by Biden despite having launched aggressive personal attacks against him in the Democratic primaries, which she now explains as 'That's politics!' She has highly advertised presidential ambitions of her own. Unlike Biden, she suffers from a likeability problem.

Few believe that Joe Biden will be a high-energy leader. In the past, he has been a follower rather than a leader of the trends within his party. But since his election, he has performed well, promising a more normal and less divisive presidency. Since few expect him, by then in his eighties, to seek or win re-election, he will need to enjoy to the full his first two years as President, as after that he will risk being overshadowed by the scramble to succeed him on the part of his Vice-President and others on his own side.

The Democrats have continued to win most of the votes of the black and Hispanic minorities (though Trump won the anti-Castro votes in Florida and one third of Hispanic votes overall). But in the 2016 election Hillary Clinton lost among every category of white voters, irrespective of age or income. This, plus the job losses and stagnation of wages for blue-collar Americans, is why elections have become more polarised and hostile, as many feel that the country they thought they knew is becoming less familiar and recognisable, and the future indeed 'ain't what it used to be'. Most Americans no longer believe that their children will be better off than they are. While crowds sympathising with the victims of police brutality marched with the radical organisers of Black Lives Matter (committed to 'tearing down the system'), many others were appalled by the looting, violence and arson that accompanied many of these protests.

As for the 'culture wars', there are those like Kamala Harris who contend that the US, despite having elected then re-elected a black President, is 'systemically racist' and most of the problems of black America are the fault of white America. On the other hand, no one is supposed to mention that *75 per cent* of black Americans grow up in single-parent families, the single parent being almost always female. Or that by far the greatest threat of violence to black Americans is other black Americans. So, there are 'cultural' issues that need to be addressed on both sides.

I am a Republican, but, Joe Biden having won the

election, I do not want to see him fail. The demonstrations led the police in several cities to reduce patrolling. There has been a sharp rise in gun violence in New York and Chicago (in both of which there have been several hundred recent shootings) and in several other cities. Biden will need to do what he can to help to reverse the surge in violence.

The concern of his critics has been that Biden was being swept along in the leftward drift of the Democratic Party, with plans to vastly increase spending on Medicaid, infrastructure, green energy and minority communities and a huge increase in the size of government. But with the Republicans winning seats in the House of Representatives and likely to retain control of the Senate, he has no mandate to pursue any very leftist agenda.

The Democrats also were contemplating creating extra seats on the Supreme Court to pack it with 'progressives'. The liberal icon Ruth Bader Ginsburg warned against this on the grounds that the other side would then do the same, devaluing the Supreme Court and turning it into a political football. This too may need to be put on hold. The electorate voted for the moderate, not the supposedly radical, version of Joe Biden. In the quarrel between moderate and 'progressive' Democrats, he has so far come out firmly as the moderate most of those who elected him believe him to be.

There is plenty President Biden could do that we could all applaud. Like stopping the new technology companies, who have been schmoozing him shamelessly, paying so pathetically small an amount in taxes and trying to escape regulation and crush competition wherever they can. And the US tax system does need to be reformed to prevent billionaires (not only Donald Trump but all of them) paying so little in taxes in relation to their wealth.

So what reason is there to be cheerful? No one ever yet did well betting against the United States. The US economy will revive, more strongly than most others. No one can govern America for long from too far to the left or right. Our politicians are going to have to re-discover that reality and will find that bi-partisanship on some issues was not such a bad idea. Joe Biden says that he will try to reach agreement with some of his opponents across the aisle. If he wants to succeed in his limited tenure as President, as we all should hope he will, he is going to need to really try to make politics less partisan and confrontational. He can succeed by showing that, this time around, he is a leader not a follower and, as Bill Clinton did, that he has the resolve to stand up to some of his own radical, hyper-activist supporters.

AFTERWORD: A FEW LESSONS LEARNED

So, these have been my solutions to life after the White House. Do I feel some nostalgia? Of course I do, for having worked for – to me – a great President, who is now recognised as such. But for politics in general, the partisanship and frantic climbing up the greasy pole only to fall back down again, not at all. I am very fortunate to have had the experiences I have enjoyed, and am extremely grateful to the many who have helped me, though I did also have to make my own efforts to experience the universe beyond Muncie, Indiana. There is no need whatsoever to end up holidaying on the Riviera; I would be just as happy doing so in a log cabin on Lake Leelanau (close to where Madonna hails from), though my cow-tipping days sadly are over. It is enjoying the journey that counts, and if you are not then try to change direction, as I have had to do a time or two. Ambition and talent are fine, but likeability is important too. Never be dismayed at starting from the bottom, as effort plus enthusiasm normally will ensure that you don't stay there. Meanwhile, I hope that one or two of you will follow my example in laying siege to the White House – and then deciding that there are even better things to do in life thereafter.

ACKNOWLEDGEMENTS

I am extremely grateful to James Stephens and Lucy Stewardson at Biteback Publishing and to Douglas Cooper for their invaluable help with the publication of this memoir. For help with the pictures, I am indebted especially to my mother Judy Bracken, to Leah Wangarim and to the excellent photographer Loic Bisoli.

INDEX